ANCHOR BOOKS

HORSES GALORE

First published in Great Britain in 1993 by
ANCHOR BOOKS
1-2 Wainman Road, Woodston,
Peterborough, PE2 7BU

Foreword

Anchor Books is a small press, established in 1992, with the aim of promoting readable Poetry to as wide an audience as possible.

We hope to establish an outlet for writers of Poetry who may have struggled to see their work in print.

Following our request in the National Press, we were overwhelmed by the response. The poems presented here have been selected from many entries. Editing proved to be a difficult and daunting task and, as the Editor, the final selection was mine.

The Poems chosen represent a cross-section of styles and content. They have been sent from all over the country, written by young and old alike united in the passion for writing poetry.

I trust this selection will delight and please the authors and all those who enjoy reading poetry.

Contents

Beauty of the Horse	Eve Romeril	1
Just a Loving Memory	Emma Greaney	2
The Horse - A Tribute	Janet Winter	3
I Kick	Suzanne Baylis	4
My Daughter's Pony	Marilyn Wilson	5
Our Shetland Pride	Alanda Anderson	6
Spanish Mane	Karen Lilburn	7
The Pit Pony . . .	Louise Murden	8
Retirement	Jean Arber	9
Spring	Meg Young	10
Morning Spell	Caroline Rivers	11
Ben	Marion Swindell	12
Pony Club Camp	Alison McKie	13
Ricky - Spring 1988	Helen Hail	14
Magic	Sandra Bennett	15
Chelsea Girl	Lynne Ramsey	16
The Mare and Foal	Myra Clifford	17
Memories of Brandy	Linda Campbell	18
Childhood Dreams	Theresa Dakin	20
Best Turned Out Melody	Rosemary Smith	21
The Black Stallion	Sharon Harkness	22
Charge	Christine Church	23
Fella	Anthea Elvin	24
Welcome Home	Heléne Desmond	25
Musical Lady	Tanya Smith	26
Jack	Doreen Connolly	27
The Morning Ride	Anna Trenter	28
The Story of Misty	Judy Winfield	29
To a Memory	Katy Jones	30
Dreams Do Come True	Charles William Frankham	31
Colour Prejudice	Ann Hutchings	32
For Sale	Marilyn Danson	33
The Final Farewell	Abigail White	34
Mimic	Louise Brown	35
Pedro	Josephine Bocock	36
Friends for Life	Sarah Jane Owens	37

The Horse Drive	Jenny Shuttleworth	38
A Child's Dream	Penny Jones	39
The Grey Horse	Mari McLellan	40
Wishing	Helen Cutmore	41
I Imagine	Louise Revill	42
The Empty Field	Caroline Merrington	43
My Friend Piggy	Helen Pollard	44
Scooby Doo	Lisa Downham	45
The Fair	Sharon Jones	46
A Moorland Pony	Kate Robinson	47
My Little Black Mare	Dawn Kendall	48
Horses	Ebby Johnson	49
Dreamer	P J Powell	50
A Horse	Marjorie Cowan	51
Great Expectations	S Cogswell	52
Cave Painting	Kathryn Ashton	53
The Vision	Kate Hill	54
Unexpected Moments	Joanne Wilkes	55
Unobtainable	Claire Thorburn	56
White Horse/Helpless Hands	Jo Wightman	57
Spice	Lucy Edwards	58
Something Dark and Real	Jacquie Molyneux	59
Saracen	Cherry Brannan	60
March	Joan Calmady-Hamlyn	61
Zanti	Amanda Pollard	62
The Favourite	Bridget Sutton	63
Ode to Blue	Linda Bray	64
A Rodent in Disguise	Jacqueline Hambrook	65
The Wait	Joanne Crossley	66
My Dream Horse	Cheryl Gamble	67
Jimmy my Highland Pony	Pauline Ward	68
Phantom Horse	Lisa Jayne Bronger	69
The Horse	Susan Murray	70
Transformation	Leigh Duncan	71
Cloudy	Louise V Pearson	72
A Horse Talk	Marie-Francoise Frossard	73
Jimmy's Lament	Hazel McKendrick	74
The Show Pony	Sarah Bushe	75

A Wonderful Gift	Karen O'Driscoll	76
The Foal	Brenda Foxcroft	77
Searching for Skewbald Polly!	Janis R Witt-Way	78
My Pony Minnie	Karen Bosworth	79
Let us Salute the Horse!	Liz Morrison	80
Misty the Race Horse	Sarah Whitehead	81
Galloping . . .	Samantha Rodwell	82
The Jumping Two	Jaime Towers	83
Thomas	Michelle Ball	84
He's Gem (a Tribute)	Elaine Bird	85
Day One	Sharon Kerr	86
Dancing Willow - What a Nice Name!	Rachel Westbury	87
The Show	Sharon Lee	89
Whoever Named Her Snowie?	Jackie Alexander	90
Bred to Win	Barbara Bancroft	91
The Thoroughbred	Carol Jones	92
Ode to Conker	Hayley Brown	93
The Black Stallion	Tania Day	94
The Wild Horses	Julia Parker	95
Ecofisk Foxtrot - (or Timmy for short)	Joyce M Hollows	96
Buzby	Carolyn Archer	97
Horses for Courses	Emma Nielsen	98
The Horse	Caroline Couldwell	100
Perfect Ride	Christina Urso-Cale	101
Back to Work	D Pratt	102
Dreams do Come True	Sharron Elizabeth Merrills	103
The Arabian Horse	Elizabeth Fowler	104
A Horse's Beauty	Debbie Gradwell	105
The Horse	Aimee Gasston	106
Babs the Best	Emma Young	107
Soloman Grundy	Vickie Clay	108
Dark Horse	Mary Reed	109
Urgent Journey	Jan McIntosh	110

Beauty of the Horse

The flowing beauty of the horse,
As his fiery hooves gallop free,
The land his own.
His blazing glory shines out high,
As he roams the hills,
But the hills become fields,
The lands become towns,
The real beauty of the horse is gone,
He can roam no more,
But still his bold nature lives on,
His spirit remains,
No longer free but tamed,
Man's servant for time to come,
His enchantment is ruled by our wishes,
The pure magic lives no more,
It is but fantasy magic, alone.

Eve Romeril

Just a Loving Memory

A relationship that whispers words of peace,
As a bright silver tear lights up my heart.
The secret sound of enchanting happiness . . .
All just a loving memory.

The swift sound of beating hooves excites my weary soul,
As one sad silver tear sings a forbidden melody.
I rub my hands along his neck . . .
All just a loving memory.

His deep breathing on my shoulder,
His sweet eyes burning bright,
As one last silver tear chokes my happy soul . . .
The mists of darkness fills my heart . . .
The torturous memories burn my soul . . .
All just a loving memory.

Emma Greaney (13)

The Horse - A Tribute

Mystery and majesty combined with grace,
are found throughout the equine race.
Strength and beauty go hand in hand,
with courage and patience in their service to man.
All through history they have been to the fore,
carrying man; so bravely through countless battles and war.
As transport, in industry, agriculture, and down the mines,
the horse is truly one of a kind.
So many breeds, so versatile,
and each with its own unique style.
Now its days as a workhorse are in the past,
the horse has turned to other tasks.
Today his talents are seen in sport and leisure,
giving millions so much pleasure.

Janet Winter

I Kick

'Watch out! I kick!'
Said the horse to the rider,
With a ferocious glare.

Still the rider took no notice,
Yet was very soon aware,
Of a horse that told him that he kicked.
So Beware! Beware! Beware!

Suzanne Baylis

4

My Daughter's Pony

My Daughter's Pony's name is King,
He really is the most gorgeous thing,
With ears pricked up and tail held high,
Around the field he loves to fly,
His coat is soft and satin smooth,
His mane and tail shimmer like silver too,
In Winter his coat is fluffy and white,
But in Summer its cream and a beautiful sight,
If in earlier times he had been born,
I'm sure he would have been Pegasus or a Unicorn.

Marilyn Wilson

Our Shetland Pride

On a Shetland hill so calm and still
Stands a pony free at will
With a bushy tail and flowing mane
No-one really knows his name
With his shaggy coat and unshod feet
And other ponies near to meet
What a life for this little 'Sheltie'
With shelter scarce but food of plenty
The tourists come with cameras flashing
To watch this pony so brave and dashing
No wonder we look and fill with pride
To see our ponies so free and wild.

Alanda Anderson

Spanish Mane

Take the ribbon from your mane.
Shake it loose and let it fall.
Neck arched, mane cascading,
Like on a crest of a wave.
For all to adore.
Silver body, perfectly toned, shimmering in the light,
Looking like a perfect suit of armour shining in the night.
Each leg perfectly shaped, to support,
Such an elegant body of contained power
But moves so light
His head so intelligent, kind and even courageous
So proud he stands to his full height.
The Andalucian captivates his audience,
Almost hypnotising them with his charm and character.
He is sure a perfect delight.

Karen Lilburn

The Pit Pony . . .

I awoke to the sound of banging metal,
In walked a man, black as death.
I struggled as he put on my harness
As he dragged me out,
Out to the sound of banging metal.

I walked out to the choking of dust,
Being dragged by black as death.
I walked towards a cart of coal
Piled high and ten tons heavy,
Out in the choking of dust.

I was strapped to the front of the cart,
Then whipped with a wooden rod.
I heaved at the cart
And barely moved it,
Strapped to the front of the cart.

Louise Murden

Retirement

Stand still old horse,
Stand dosing in the sun.
Fear not the thought of death
Now that your work is done.

Stand still old horse,
Remember all the fun,
When we rode out in the morning mists
And canter in the sun.

Stand still old horse
And dream of things to be,
Hay, Grass, a warm deep bed
Large fields to roam in free.

Stand still old horse,
The best is yet to be,
Oh I'll make sure that your alright
Who once took care of me.

Jean Arber

Spring

Morning, and down to the yard to feed the horses.
Bird-song fills the air, heralding the longed-for arrival of Spring.
New life surges once more, fulfilling the eternal promise.

Sun-stroked, we set out for our daily exercise, my horse
Jauntily stepping out along the country lane.
Breezes blow briskly, scudding clouds across the sky.

Menacingly, a large black polythene bag flaps in the greening
                                               hedgerow.
Fearful of what he does not understand, the grey horse stops
Dead, until persuaded, by his trust in the wisdom of man, to pass.

'Only a polythene bag' I say, reassuringly.
But is he right to fear it? It represents
Progress, modern farming, bringing a disregard for the natural order.

The horse fears what he does not understand.
Man understands and is recklessly unafraid,
Immediate advantage outweighing all else.

Can we destroy the eternal promise of Spring?

Meg Young

Morning Spell

It's early morning, the scene is set,
The sun is rising, the ground is wet.
The sun's hesitant rays touch the ground,
As the beauty of nature lies all around.
A dappled flank and toss of head,
A clink of bit, but nothing is said.
An understanding between the two,
As strong hooves break through the dew.
The sound of hoofbeats, sure and strong,
The draw of breath, sweet and long.
The bluebell woods and disused well,
Are all part of this magic spell.
The world has stopped for nothing moves,
Except the pounding of his quickening hooves.
The strides are long and full of strength,
The sun gains intensity, its rays more length.
The dew has gone, and so has the dream,
And all that flows now is the wood's small stream.
The early morning's escape ends once more,
But they'll come back - it's nature's law.

Caroline Rivers

Ben

To see our Ben as I first saw him,
You'd wonder why we ever bought him.
He'd stood for months in a dealers pen,
All fat and hairy was our Ben.
He had no shoes, was very fresh,
When sat upon - off he'd dash!
But as I stood and looked at him
He stared straight back with a knowing grin.
He knew as I did that we'd find,
Beneath the exuberance a horse so kind.
That now we've had him almost a year,
He's become a patient friend so dear.
He hunts, he hacks and show jumps too,
He's quiet to clip, to box and shoe.
And looking back to when I first saw him,
I know now why I ever bought him.
Although a novice four just then,
He's now mature and five - is Ben.

Marion Swindell

12

Pony Club Camp

Pony Club Camp, soon will come,
All those days with nothing but fun.
My pony Amanda, and all our tack
Not forgetting my Jods and my Riding Hat.
I can't wait until August 4th
The day we will be setting off.
Another week of fun and pleasure
Let's just pray for good weather.
When that day comes (I wish it would hurry)
The day before will be a scurry.
The Mini Gymkhana on the last day,
The evenings galloping on my beautiful bay.
The days of those lectures, how interesting they get
Often followed by a wonderful trek
Oh I wish those days soon would come,
No more school but loads of fun.

Alison McKie

Ricky - Spring 1988

Big grey hunter
pass into the damp grey mists of Dunkery.
gallop, forever free.
No other will ever overtake you now,
nor could they in your heyday.
That quickening and sudden surge of power,
an exhilaration I'll always love you for

And for the resting form in the night stable,
legs and hoofed tucked neatly round,
who didn't mind another moving close.

Power tamed, yet never enslaved.
You were cantankerous near the end,
when ridden or close to others of your kind,
but always affable and gentle to be led
up to your high pasture and set free.
Now, pass into the damp grey mists of Dunkery,
big grey hunter.

Helen Hail

Magic

He was just a little fellow when I first set eyes on him,
Coltish brown body atop legs elegant and slim.
Eyes full of mischief, or innocence of gaze,
Ears eager, listening, to the sounds of hectic days.

Over stable door he thrust an enquiring nose,
To nibble an apple, or the fingers of those
Who expected good manners and got youthful zeal!
Manners come later - Youth samples by feel!

Stand by the gate to see him prancing
With the spirit of Freedom - a wild careless dancing.
Hooves flying skyward, neck arched in proud line,
Such elegant beauty - such bearing so fine!

How tall he grew in the Spring's dewy flight,
Flew wild about in the warm Summer light
Which shone on his neck as he tossed his head -
Then off, scattering daisies from their grassy bed!

Sandra Bennett

Chelsea Girl

Chelsea was my horse, my friend
her memory I hold dear.
The good, the bad the times we had
no other horse could come near.
But Chelsea left one parting gift
her handsome little son.
Good times will start again for sure
and so will all the fun.
The foal cannot replace my mare
but I'm hoping he will try.
I loved her and I miss her still
Why did she have to die?

Lynne Ramsey

The Mare and Foal

Silent and still, I lay in the clearing,
grass.rippling gently all around me
caught in the early evening breeze,
hoping my patience would be rewarded.
Then, here they are, a familiar yet thrilling sight.
The Mare and Foal.
She, the colour of night itself,
and the little one,
clothed with the sun's white rays,
splashed with memories of the night:-
black on white.
She stands snorting the humid air around
while he comes closer,
then closer again - curiosity aroused.
Soon he's here beside me,
patience rewarded, joy inside.
His jet black, velvet muzzle fits in the curve of my palm.
His neat hooves stamp imperiously on the dry ground.
He wants all attention,
from the tips of his sharp ears
to white wispy foals tail.
Then he rears,
bantering playfully with the air;
then is gone
as his dam turns and calls him,
they leave,
a very special moment to keep.
Moments usually found in dreams I've weaved.

Myra Clifford

Memories of Brandy

You filled my days with happy times
My childhood filled with pleasure
and of these times I think so much
These memories I shall treasure.

Of bareback riding through the fields
Of jumping and gymkhana
Of pouring rain and whistling winds
The things we did together.

Of long long rides upon the moors
Of gallops on the beach
Of all the things you gave to me
the lessons you did teach.

My nose pressed close into your neck
The smell and sweet aroma
Your cheeky eyes and cheeky face
No one could ever take your place.

Your gentle whicker as you heard my steps
My great excitement the day we met
The very few times you had the vet.

Of all the times that I fell off
And all the times you never ran off
You never bucked reared or kicked
How glad I am it was you I picked.

We were the best of pals how I loved you so
It broke my heart to see you go
I remember you well after all these years
All the days you worked and tried to serve.

Although my childhood's long since gone
My memories of you Brandy linger on.

Linda Campbell

Childhood Dreams

Through my childhood dreams
You would gallop every day
Now many years later
At last, you're here to stay.

Adult now, I may be
More sensible and wise
But you look as I imagined
Through those childish eyes.

I loved you when I dreamt you
I loved you at first glance
I want to love you always
And now I have the chance.

You've been hurt by others in the past
But you chose me somehow
And the fun we thought had passed us by
Will be ours to savour now.

You're not an equine superstar
Your assets often go unseen
But you're more than I had hoped for
My horse, my love, my dream.

Theresa Dakin

Best Turned Out Melody

Although Melody is beginning to get old,
She loves going to all the local shows.
Best Turned Out is the class we like to do,
So it is very annoying, when she loses a shoe.

One day she looked the peak of perfection,
Her plaits went just right, no dandruff in sight.
With all the right gear, all cleaned like new,
We travelled along admiring the view.

We got up at five, to be there by nine,
Prompt said the programme, please be on time.
'This way' called Tracey 'I've just seen it signed'
The village we're looking for is not hard to find.

We travelled along with pony behind
Oh! she did look nice, as if in her prime.
We arrived at the location, then had a great shock
The show had been cancelled, the gate fixed with a lock.

'Too Wet' said the notice displayed in the field
Along the path that we should have wheeled.
No Judge saw Melody looking her best,
She wanted to stand along with the rest.

Feeling upset and tired, we couldn't feel worse
About the day that Melody may have come *first*

Rosemary Smith

The Black Stallion

The Black Stallion roams free,
His only shelter is a tree,
No-one can catch him and ride him tame,
And make this beauty rich with fame,
His food is grass,
His water sea,
He is as free, as free as can be.

Sharon Harkness

Charge

Riding boots bright and clean
With that unused shining gleam
Gleefully striding out anticipation in the air
On this morning, fresh horses with us to bear
Land and trees stetching far
This really is better than a convertible car.

'Are you happy to gallop' I was asked
As the leader's horse friskily went past
With legs gripping hard I made some sort of sign
And told 'Hold on to his mane and you will be fine'
Laughing he knows just what to say
He knew it wasn't my very first day.

Off we went at such a dash
Honest I don't care if I am last
Mud shooting up from under hooves
I don't think a mud face pack is what I would choose
Eyes watering as we reach the trees
With cheeks glowing bright from the breeze.

That really was brilliant we smile with joy
Can we have a second go please Roy?

Christine Church

Fella

Seven years ago you came to us,
The very best day of our lives,
You brought us so much pleasure
But we're left with tears in our eyes.

We loved you so very dearly
And you loved us in return,
Taking good care of the children
Every day your keep you'd earn.

You carried us all oh so safely
Just for fun or for a prize
Everyone loved and relied on you
But we're left with tears in our eyes.

In all those seven years dear Fella
You never put a foot wrong
With nose poking out and ears a-pricked
You'd just keep trotting along.

But sadly you're no longer with us
And there the heartache lies,
For you passed away last Tuesday
And we're left with tears in our eyes.

The light has gone out from the field now
We miss you and still love you so.
But you've earnt your rest, dear Fella,
And we must learn to let go.

Anthea Elvin

Welcome Home

In the night, I can feel my little
mountain of boulders,
rise by my right shoulder.
Half way along the flooded gravel track,
- is something black.
With ears cocked and tail drumming,
sits my sentinel dog.
See the rushes bending. The mist
softly creeps into collar and shoe.
Here come my ponies,
jumping ditches in the dark!
Greeting me with certainty.
My tame moon glows upon the thatch,
showing me the green door and the latch,
- then reels across the silent bog.

Heléne Desmond

Musical Lady

Musical Lady is her registered name,
Her ancestry is full of fame,
The red shine of her coat without a mark,
As you can tell she has stolen my heart.

And when she is running out free in the grass,
Her head proud and fine wise eyes shining like glass,
I now know that I will not be alone,
for wherever she is that will be my home.

No matter what hardships I have to face,
I know I can do it for I have a place,
That's out running free in the sun, wind and rain
When I'm with my horse there is no pain.

And out in the place is where I love to be
Just Musical Lady the woods and me.

Tanya Smith

Jack

I hear them calling my name Jack
I just ignore them and wont look back
In my field I want to stay
with the others I like to play.

I prefer being in here and having a roll
or peering over the fence at the new foal.

Sometimes it's nice when we go out on a hack
Especially when I have on my clean tack
A bird flies out I don't jump at that
because basically I'm much too laid back.

Oh no it's lesson time this morning
They might enjoy it but I find it boring.

Here comes mother and daughter to ride me again
mother's riding can be a bit of a pain
her leg shoots forward I don't know what to do
so I think perhaps I'll canter off with you.

But now I must say her riding's improving
she uses her leg and gets me moving.

I don't mind the daughter as she's very good
she rides me well as show knows she should.

The ride is over they say well done Jack
but I'm thinking just get off my back.

Let me go in the stable and eat my hay
next to my neighbour Quest the bay.

Doreen Connolly

27

The Morning Ride

Riding solitary one early June morning,
A young girl and her pony,
The horizon seemed limitless.
Goosegrass nodded its brittle lace in the glassy light,
And among the chestnut trees a blackbird splintered the sky with
song.

Drunk with the promise of that Summer day
Child and pony galloped heedlessly,
Their hoofbeats muffled in the tangled grass
And after, exulting, lords of the world,
Shouted joy to the laughing sun.
The child unknowing that the memory, painfully sweet,
Would return unlooked for when pony and child were gone.

Anna Trenter

The Story of Misty

I first saw Misty at a local sale
Forlorn and miserable she stood alone
Waiting to be sold,
Not long parted from her foal.
She was walked and trotted up and down
So well behaved we thought,
So we did bid and we did win
The man across the yard.
So chuffed were we
And excitedly shook with glee,
I paid my dues, and then collected our
New addition from her pen.
She loaded with unexpected ease
Like she'd done it all before
I got her home and then with ease,
Unloaded her and set her free.
Into her field she did go
Please to see the grass,
Straight away she ate her fill
Enjoying all the tastes
This was two years ago
And now we find
A bigger family have we,
For Misty was again in foal
And now Rio is here for all to see.
So, this is the story of Misty
The twenty-one year old OAP,
But far from looking forlorn and worn,
Now she too is filled with glee.

Judy Winfield

To a Memory

(Dedicated to Kim, a beautiful horse and friend who died in a thunder storm. With thanks to her for all she taught me, and to the Hagues for letting me ride her.)

I still remember our meeting was it really five years?
Struck by your awesome beauty, full of wonder and fears.
The blind led the blind, we strove, battled and cried,
You were my strength and I your guide.
Moving forward as one everywhere together,
Not just horse and rider, understanding each other.
Fences paled beneath you gliding on glory.
Hours were spent just swapping stories!
Tragically taken from me as lightning struck one night,
I still see it, blackness, storms and fright.
Such a violent death ripped our souls apart,
God hadn't considered my broken heart
I couldn't even face horses, not again,
The pleasure and pride wiped out by pain.
But they're in my blood, what do they say?
'Life goes on, seize the day'
So there's a new young mare - fiery chestnut,
Certainly a challenge to relish, but . . .
I'll never forget you darling, I hope you think of me,
I picture you now in heaven, at last, wild and free.

Katy Jones

30

Dreams Do Come True

I always dream of competing in show jumping although, I've never
been
I have my own pony called Sabrina but she's not very keen
She gallops around in her field she's really full of go
But when it comes to jumping she doesn't want to know.
I school her every chance I get I am sure she has the scope
I always start by lunging her on a piece of rope
I really don't know what to do I'm at my wits end
For if Sabrina doesn't jump I'll go around the bend
But perhaps one day she'll change her mind
With a lot of fuss and a little bit of time
But until then I can only dream
Of Sabrina and I as a brilliant team.
People say some dreams do come true
So I keep telling Sabrina, there's still hope for you.
My practising and schooling were for the best
For Sabrina and I is a big success.
So other riders who's ponies aren't willing
Dreams do come true I bet you a shilling
And other riders you'd better watch out
We're worthy rivals without any doubt.

(The late)

Charles William Frankham

31

Colour Prejudice

There are poems about ponies, pure shining white
There's stories of horses, black as the night
There are poems of ponies, gold like the sun
There's even a tale of a two coloured one.

There's poems of ponies burnished like brass
Of dapple grey ponies, turned out to grass
Stories of horses of dark iron grey
And loads whose hero's turn out to be bay.

But I've never read a single one
About a pony that's *dun*

Ann Hutchings

For Sale

He won't box, he doesn't jump
And has been known to nap,
His feet are prone to crumbling,
He may have pulled a trap.
He's difficult to catch at times
Costs too much to keep
And if I find the time to ride
He always seems asleep.
We're only asking a few hundred pounds, really not a lot,
We simply must get shot of him, because we've bought a shop.

He does box, he loves to jump,
His feet now look A1
I've had him almost five years now
And when I call he'll come.
He never naps, enjoys his food,
We ride out every day,
And each time that I look at him I think of what they say . . .
He won't box, he doesn't jump
And has been known to nap
And I wonder if those people knew
Just what a super chap
They had 'for sale'

Marilyn Danson

33

The Final Farewell

His hooves like thunder shook the deserted moor,
His broad black back was arched, whether in joy or defiance
she was not sure.
His muscles rippled like an ocean wave,
And his nostrils were enflamed and as deep as caves.
His breath was white as white as snow,
But he galloped on led by the moon's watchful glow.
His breath like smoke rose and danced in the icy night,
His eyes were like jewels, sparkling bright.
He was more powerful than evil,
Yet as graceful as a feather,
His body was like iron, his paces hell for leather.
His silhouette like a phantom drifted by his side,
And he was the perfect image of stallion pride.
His tail seemed to sway to a beat of its own,
The horse had a mission, a mission alone.
He slid back into darkness as quickly as he came,
And she knew now she would never see him again.
Her beloved horse who had passed away life,
Had now discovered an existence without pain or strife.
Yet just once had he returned as a gesture of farewell,
To thank her for caring through those last days of hell.
She smiled through her tears as she realised with mirth,
He was destined to gallop 'til the ends of the earth.

Abigail White (15)

Mimic

Her eyes are flames of freedom,
her coat is shining fine
Golden wings are on her heels,
and a string of streams behind her.

Her eyes are pools of darkness
with pupils made of fire,
She gazes at everything in sight,
her trotting steps are gay and light.

Her coat is golden fire,
with sunlight glazing,
and as she floats across the field,
her beauty is amazing.

Her mane, swift as the wind,
In all her young delight
elegant and beautiful,
Prancing fire and light.

Her white socks flash in the light
a pennant tail behind her,
with head flung high up in the air,
as nothing can be wilder.

Louise Brown (13)

Pedro

Thanks my friend for the moments we shared,
Treasured moments when our minds thought alike.
Thanks for your wonderful greetings
My great companion and comforter
Thanks for your stillness when watching partridge chicks
For the pleasure of seeing mad March hares boxing,
Thanks for the memory of the lithe stoat chasing his tail
For all the wildlife you told me about.

Many is the hour we spent together,
My skewbald friend and I.
We travelled miles, a well known pair,
Up hill, down vale, along tracks and roads
The pleasure of a paddle in the sea
A gallop on the beach
From showing to hunting, games to social rides
We tried them all.

We rode to meet the dawn
We rode off into the sunset
We raced for the gold at the end of the rainbow
We rode by the silvery moon
We lazed on hot Summers' days
You grazing, while I read under the willow trees.

You so steady, yet eager and enthusiastic
So polite, gentle and careful
The greatest honour you bestowed upon me
Allowing me to ride you free in the field
No saddle, no bridle, no halter
Just you and me, my friend cantering free.

Josephine Bocock

Friends for Life

The first time I saw you,
Asleep in your bed of straw,
You were but a baby,
Wide eyed and so unsure.

At first you didn't trust me,
Wary of every deed,
But now our friendship's growing
Like a plant from tiny seed.

Now that Winter's passing,
And Summer's on the way,
I've watched you growing stronger,
Learning more each day.

Our bond is slowly forming,
Being cast like solid steel,
Once forged it's never broken,
For you it's what I feel.

When I'm welcomed with a whinny
And your joy is clear to see,
You trot up to the gate,
I know your love belongs to me.

Sarah Jane Owens

The Horse Drive

The sun brightly clothes this country place,
Swollen and vibrant for one week of the year.
The Mecca of travellers, the magnet of dreams.
The heart of the culture, the blood of their life.

I round the crook of the river's sheltering arm
To where it enters the slow-stream current under the bridge.
And there I stand, gape, gasp, and marvel
At its transformation to turbulent seas.

Seventeen patched and coloured horses pound down the bank,
Laced together with twine and rope.
Crack open the sleeping waters with giant movements
So basking trout boil in white crested waves.
Down, down they go, till all in a line
The horses plunge and swim downstream, urged on by a tiny gypsy
child
Clinging to the neck of the greatest beast.
Aloft, other boys hold bottles of detergent
Squirting emerging rumps and backs with snakes of green.
Rubbing and patting, smacking and whooping,
In and out, darting and diving, dicing with death
In the raging waters, turned white with foam.
On, on the regiment drives, under the bridge
At a water-impeded slow motion gallop,
To the far grassy bank on the other side.
Gleaming and dripping, the pounding stops
As, Indian like, the horses emerge and immediately graze.
The barefoot sodden waif, still perched, hoots in triumph
As his army gather ranks for the Appleby sale.

Jenny Shuttleworth

38

A Child's Dream

He may be small, the hands don't count,
His size is right for me to mount,
Upon my horse I take my rein,
and point my steed towards the lane.
No shows today or hills to climb
Just a hack to pass the time,
Movement is slight my journey has started,
together forever, never to be parted.
A lifetime together and joys abound,
No horse so gracious could ever be found
Always, forever,
His dreams will be mine,
Always and forever
My rocking horse of pine.

Penny Jones

The Grey Horse

The swift grey horse was as fast as lightening,
He pounded his hooves, it seemed quite frightening
His head carried high, and his tail so fine,
I wish so much that the grey horse was mine.

I saw him again at the local show
His rider, so perfect from head to toe
He made no movement, he's as good as gold
His rider sitting tall, she looked so bold.

As they entered the ring, silence arose
His legs were all in line, his 'show ring pose'
They walked around the ring, she tried to steer him
She had no control, he started rearing.

They walked out of the show ring in disgrace
A sad look upon the young rider's face
His tail between his legs, his head so low
He is not very good, but now I know.

Mari McLellan

Wishing

I wish I had that horse
Who's name is Mr Mac
But I know I won't of course
Because my mum doesn't like jet black.

I would groom him every night
And ride him every day
His coat would shine so bright
Everyone would say

What a lovely little pony
With his head up so high
He's not at all boney
And he doesn't even shy.

Helen Cutmore

I Imagine

I imagine a dark open field,
There is another being
About in all its happiness
About in all its loneliness.

While mist is laden on its bed,
It approaches me slowly, wearily.
Its footsteps are heard long and loud.
What can this being be?

The steps get quicker,
Quicker, Quicker.
Now stopped dead as can be
Just some misty eyes, looking back at me.

Smoke is appearing from its nose,
It looks angry, mad even.
Will it charge?
No just look and sniff.

I caught a whiff of the stench
It was a horse
But not just one though
More footsteps are heard.

Just pounding in my head,
I wake up in the morning
With a hoofprint
On my bed.

Louise Revill

The Empty Field

The grey dampness of the February morning
Clung to my cold face and hands.
I stared at the empty field,
Alone but for memories, which jostled and pushed
Causing wild confusion to race round in my head.
I was aware of a great sense of loneliness,
An emptiness that left me numb.

The rails edged the field in the familiar manner,
The barn still nestled in the hollow by the stream.
The muddy headcollar hung from my trembling hand,
The smell of manure rose from the steaming muck pile.

'Sophie' I called, but my words went unanswered,
No nicker of welcome from my four legged friend.
No thunder of hooves as she raced over to see me,
No muzzle pressed deep in the palm of my hand.

The grey dampness of the February morning
Clung to my cold face and hands.
I stared at the empty field,
Alone, but for memories.

Caroline Merrington

My Friend Piggy

At Cambridge Sales I first saw you
And thought you looked rather grand
I said to my daughter 'You know dear
I think I will raise my right hand'
'He's yours' said the man with the hammer
'Oh Dad what have you done'
Thus started a friendship
Rewarding with plenty of fun.

Now you have changed your jockey
From Katie to Becky P
I wonder how much longer you will remember me.

You will always be our little mate
Who runs to meet us at the gate
So cheers and have some extra hay
For you are ten years old today.

Helen Pollard

Scooby Doo

He's big bay and beautiful
And is like a teddy bear
He's cool, calm and collected
And never gives a care
He moves his little nostrils
And makes a little mutter
He goes into his stable
And waits there for his supper.

Lisa Downham

The Fair

Have you ever been
At the horse fair scene
Where horses are bought from under the hammer,
Hacks, Hunters, Cobs not forgetting the Vanner,
'Mind your backs' the riders cry
'Coming through' as they fly by
Horses show their hitched up skills
All gleaming coats and carts with frills
bargaining hands now start to meet
Potential new owners take the driving seat
I ask to ride the coloured Cob Mare
I'd love to have her, but should I dare
She's light in the hand, moves away from leg well
She's the one for me, I can just tell
We chatted a while, soon the deal was struck
Tack was bought, and hire of a truck
The journey home was of pure delight
Stable waiting to rest for the night.

Sharon Jones

A Moorland Pony

His head held high
His ears pricked forward
He has sighted the mares he wants
But . . .
There is the stallion
He will have to fight.

The stranger comes at him
In full flight
The stranger is bigger
The stranger is stronger
The stranger is going to win
The screams are shrill
The stranger won

Now for our pony it's back to square one.

Kate Robinson

My Little Black Mare

I have a little black mare,
Who has rather a lot of hair.
She once rolled off on two pairs of skates,
And ended up at a pretty tall gate.
Which she tried to jump,
But landed with a bump
In a bunch of prickly thorns.
She was all tangled up
Like a spikey hedgehog
And I had to cut her free.
But she was really unhappy,
Because she was very knotty.
So in the end she drove me round the bend
And I clipped her right out.
I still have a little black mare
But she's now got rather short hair.

Dawn Kendall

Horses

H is for happy because that is what my pony makes me.
O is for over, jumping jumps as high as can be.
R is for rain when I have to ride, to show him I care.
S is for silly when he spooks and gives me a scare.
E is for envious because that's what people are of us.
S is for *simply the best* to have a beautiful pony that I can trust.

Ebby Johnson (14)

Dreamer

We haven't been together very long
Everyone said the partnership was wrong
My grey tornado as fast as light
Hold on, hold on, with all your might.
'Too forward going, he's much to fast
For you to ride - it cannot last.'
Riding the lanes at walk and trot
Sometimes with pleasure, often with not
Much to learn, no canter as yet
Slowly but surely, we'll get there I bet
Time to learn to get to know each other
Dreamer and I we go together.

P J Powell

A Horse

A beast of dignity and grace,
Watch his canter at steady pace
Quietly grazing in fields so green,
At times with mare and foal is seen

A racing horse with spanking pace
Even at jumps he bounds with grace!
At riding school, with children to train
A gentle trot with them at rein.

In all his moods, so fine and tall,
An animal that's loved by all.

Marjorie Cowan

51

Great Expectations

She's keeping me waiting, I know what she's at,
Her huge belly is foal, not, I hope, too much fat.
I check her thrice daily and note udder size
And she looks at me knowingly, a glint in her eyes.
I'm getting exhausted with the nightly watch too,
Just in case she's in trouble, in the dark, in the dew.
I'm sure it might happen when we're all out at work,
If I miss the event it will drive me berserk.
Eleven months patience has now worn a bit thin,
'She might yet go twelve,' said the vet with a grin.
Her own mother produced her one morning at ten.
And allowed many to witness the wondrous birth then.
This mare is quite different, I've known from the start,
And she'll plan her own timing, I must own that's she's smart.
As long as she keeps well we won't interfere,
Only realise some miracles take a whole year.

S Cogswell

Cave Painting

Across unnumbered centuries he stares,
A sandy horse upon a rocky plain
Dark muzzle seeking, tasting the restless air.
Broad neck, dark crested, arched, small ears aquiver
For hint of footfall cross a grassy sea.
Alert, one hoof half-lifted, poised for flight
Yet motionless, child of the earth and wind
Held thralled by picture magic for the hunter's spear.

Far kin to hunter/artist, I stare back
In wonder at the skill that sought to bind
The Spirit Horse to flight the homing spear.
Till sorcery stirs, he lives and through the chill
I feel upon my skin the hay-sweet breath, and I
Am held, not knowing who is hunter or who prey,
Our life entwined. And then, heart deep, I know
Why hunter tamed the wind and built a world.

Kathryn Ashton

The Vision

I stop, I stare, as I see a black blur whizz past me,
Across the lush green field,
It's faster than the wind.

I wait a while and then see it charging back,
It seems to float on the security of the mud beneath it.

The grey bath shaped tub,
In the corner of the field waits motionless
To be emptied sip after sip.

The horse is not yet tired after darting
Across the field like a train out of control at full speed.

The hair on its head,
Flows freely like fire burning a forest.

It comes to a halt,
And stares at me,
Like it was unaware that I was watching,
It runs to the grey tub and laps up the water.

Kate Hill

Unexpected Moments

Along a busy beaten track,
I take my young horse out.
Knowing I may unexpect,
A few things that may count.
We take a steady walk
By children, cars n' lorries,
Not an eyelid did she flap,
And took it in her stride.

I thought that I was lucky
To take a young horse out.
Who didn't mind,
The noise and speed,
Of passing cars and bikes.
But as we passed a single hedge,
A Blackbird flapped its wings;
And backing off, she cantered off,
Back down the way we'd been.

Keeping calm, I steadied her,
Understanding every need,
That we must turn around to carry on as though;
We had never seen,
That Blackbird in the hedgerow.
But as she nervously pottered by,
I couldn't think of why;
She was frightened, of a bird
When cars and lorries
Didn't even bother her.

Joanne Wilkes

Unobtainable

They all say they understand - I know they think they do,
But no-one knows how I feel.
'You'll be able to get another horse, when you've finished college.'
There's other horses, but there isn't him.
'Get rid of the one you've grown out of, then you can have him.'
How do you get rid of a friend?

He went to a sale, not of his own will,
He was humiliated, scrutinised, open remarks made about him,
He came back, rejected, back to his home.
Not a home.
Somewhere he stayed.
He wasn't loved. He was an object that was worth something.

I'd love him, I'd care for him.
I can look after two horses, I'd enjoy it.
'But it's the money.'
No it's not.
'Horses are expensive.'
Not in love.

I want him, I want him,
I'm slowly being tortured by undecided heartache.
He goes to another sale, comes back again.
I can't go to see him, reassure him, show him someone cared,
Because of the pain that he couldn't be mine.
Why do I fall in love with something I can't have?
Why is he so close yet hopelessly out of reach?

It's like I'm being tortured, the comings and goings.
I want him, I want him to feel cared for, I want him to know he's
                                                            loved,
I want to let him know I haven't forgotten him,
To make up for betraying him,
Please let me have him.

Claire Thorburn

White Horse/Helpless Hands

(Dedicated to the memory of Snow King)

I stare down at my hands,
The blood of life runs through them
They have served me well
Until now
Weak, useless, unable to cure him
Man can invent machines of a thousand uses,
Negotiate world peace and visit the moon.
Still I stare down at my hands
And I stare at him -
Pale and fading;
A once full moon
Now in eclipse
A spring landscape
Covered by winter
Barren, fading, strength waning.
He who gave me so much
And all I can do is watch
Crimson trickle on virgin snow.
When I close my eyes I see him
But these are stolen minutes in dreams
Only to lose him once more on waking.
His long swinging stride
The evening sunlight glinting on his back
Together we challenge the world as one
I am with him.
But in a different world.

Jo Wightman

Spice

Christmas was coming,
The goose was getting fat,
I wanted a Shetland pony,
And that was that.

I knew what to do (I thought),
I'd helped out up the stables,
It's not like school
When you've got to know your tables.

Of course there were things to learn,
With everything worthwhile there is,
My parents just thought of excuses like
It's a little girl's phase.

Since I was small
I've wanted the same thing,
And that's a Shetland pony
Then I could prove I was really caring.

If my dream ever did come true
I think it would be nice
To call the little Shetland
By the name of Spice.

Every Christmas comes and goes,
But never, does my dream,
About my little Spice the Shetland.
He will never be reality it seems.

Lucy Edwards

Something Dark and Real

Your eyes are clear
Your head is bright
I want to stay with you tonight.

You touch me like no other one
I feel with you I walk alone.
We build together
Lines of strength.
I wonder whether
You've waited lengths
For me to come.

I knew I'd hurt if you were hurt,
I know your feelings are the same.

It's like we've got so much to learn.
But I don't want to take from you.
Give me only what I earn,
And yet I know that's what you'll do.

This is not a fight
To be lost or won.
There is no right
There is no wrong,
'Tis only two who find together
Something special in each other.
Though your beauty could be sold
It's not for that your love I hold.
It's like we share the eyes of one
The simple pleasures beneath the sun.

Together we must make it happen,
Together we must remain.
I could not bear to think of you
Saddled to a distant rein.

Jacquie Molyneux

Saracen

Saracen is a beautiful horse,
He is chestnut like Bomber of course,
He's excellent in traffic and on roads,
He's fun to ride and I love him loads.
He hates some people they make him feel sick,
When he see's them he'll bite and kick.
Saracen is thoroughbred and used to race,
He is a good looker with a handsome face.
As he's still young he's sometimes bad,
But even when he is he doesn't make me sad.
Saracen's coat is shiny and fine,
One day I wish that he would be mine.

Cherry Brannan

March

The sun shone this morning
When I went round the ponies in their fields
To see them safe and sound to start another day.
The fat, bay Dartmoor mare
Stood drowsing with the early warmth upon her back
And I hoped, in two weeks time, the sun
Would shine again to warm the foal
New-dropped upon the ground.
Close by, its sturdy sire, short ears alert,
Bright eyes upon me through the tangled forelock,
Then, recognising and accepting, bent again to graze
The close-shorn grass.
But now, as I stand here once more,
The bare trees lift their stiffened branches,
Black against the pale grey sky
And evening comes. So I go home
And leave them to the night.

Joan Calmady-Hamlyn

Zanti

To me you're so special,
To my life you bring joy.
The bond that's between us
No-one could destroy.

You can sense when I'm near
You stand at your door
And as I approach
Your hoof strikes the floor.

Your black silky coat
Shines in the light.
Your big brown eyes glint
Like stars in the night.

You're the cream of the crop
To me you're the best.
And in stature and beauty
You beat all the rest.

I'm so proud to say
That you are my mount.
And of one thing I'm sure
On your love I can count.

Amanda Pollard

The Favourite

All through the winter, the favourite
Come spring the first race
Disappointment, only second,
But still, the favourite

Preparation begins in earnest for, the favourite
In a foreign land he is working,
On race day, a delay
By air he arrives, the favourite.

On toes he prances, the favourite
Will he settle? will he win?
Jockey ready, in the plate
Ready to sprint, and still the favourite

Zafonic, the favourite
Swoops to the outside
Within strides he is clear
And the winner,
        An outstanding favourite.

Bridget Sutton

Ode to Blue

After working all hours, and collecting what's due,
The momentous day finally came,
I paid my cheque, took charge of my horse,
And *Soldier Blue* was his name.

He's grey in colour and average in size,
Has a couple of fairly good paces,
He's done a bit of jumping and a bit of something else,
But I don't think he'll win any races.

We tacked up and went off happily to ride,
Not knowing what problems I'd caught,
After bucking and fighting and playing around,
I thought, 'My God what have I bought'.

With persistence and courage I carried on,
Our first show arrived with great speed,
We hacked with a friend, came first in our class,
And I congratulated my trusty steed.

Well, it's eleven years later, he's still going strong,
Perhaps a little more grey,
But still as lively and cheeky as ever,
And prefers to be grazing each day.

He's no great jumper or racer or stud,
And dressage not his favourite craze,
But he's my little horse, *the best*, of course,
And I'll keep him for the rest of his days.

Linda Bray

A Rodent in Disguise

Collect Red from his stable and Shikarah too,
Turn them both out, there's still plenty to do.
Check the field water trough and fill it if empty,
Then shake out the hay ration - yes that's plenty.
Muck out the stable and leave bed up to air,
Refill water buckets and place them just there.

Now off to the twenty acre field - carrots in pockets bulging,
To find one more horse out to grass - just now indulging.
Oh! This is a new horse, one I've only just bought
And from what my sources tell me, his life's been rather fraught
He's originally from Poland a foreigner to these parts
Accused of being headstrong as he was once pulling carts.

Here's hoping new found freedom in pastures so green
Will bring him solace from his previous homes so mean.
Some kind and firm handling that's just what he needs
To undo previous work of other human's dastardly deeds
His phobia of people has grown to immense proportion
So when entering his field - yes please take caution.

Where is he? - ah over there, he must be lying down
Don't forget his carrot or he'll greet me with a frown.
Push him or pull him and he'll show you his might
And if you try to catch him he'll just gallop out of sight
Undersaddle he's quite daunting - so please wear a hard hat.
By the way, his name is 'Roland' after TV's famous rat.

Jacqueline Hambrook

The Wait

She used to love her pony once,
but now it stands alone
half starved, forgotten in the field
a mass of skin and bone.
She liked to say, 'I've got a horse'
it seemed to quite impress
but now rather than buy some hay
she'd much prefer a dress.
Lipstick and blush replaced the craze
it's part of growing older
the pony doesn't need a rug
it isn't that much colder.
It's raining rather hard now
so she won't go to the field tonight
She fed the pony Sunday
and it seemed to be alright.
She can't go up tomorrow,
She is going to a dance
it might be a bit hungry
but she'll have to take the chance.
She can't afford to buy more feed
she's saving for a car,
it has to be one or the other
it's a shame but there you are.
What price to suffer, waiting,
endless vigil by the gate
waiting for food that never comes
with a heart that feels no hate.

Joanne Crossley

My Dream Horse

I saw the horse of my dream,
drinking from a nearby stream,
I imagined myself having a ride,
with the birds on the air trying to glide.

I stood there with a stare,
at this lovely gleaming mare,
she was covered in dappled grey,
and soon gave out a lovely neigh.

She came trotting over to me,
compared to her I looked so wee.
Suddenly I woke up and realised
that it was only a dream.

Cheryl Gamble

Jimmy my Highland Pony

Just another pony grazing in a field,
Occasionally he stands and sniffs the breeze,
Does it come from the lochs and the glens where his ancestors,
Roamed and bred and worked for years?

Just another pony, twenty one years old.
Still full of vigour and strength and beauty,
Yet so gentle, any child is safe on his back,
Looking after beginners seems to him to be a duty.

Just another pony, intelligent and cheeky,
Slipping headcollars and rolling in mud.
Following me around for the mints in my pocket.
Letting me know 'he's starving', but if I feed him he'll be good!

Just another pony, still winning prizes,
At riding club, dressage and local shows,
He can be a stubborn, cantankerous old so and so,
Yet on a hack, he's as game as any thoroughbred that goes.

Not just another pony, this is Jimmy my Highland,
Giving me his affection and love and trust,
In return I'll give him every attention,
For with me keeping Jimmy happy's a must!

Pauline Ward

Phantom Horse

With dainty hooves and a small dished face,
And yet fleet of foot and so sure,
She stands under the oak tree by post and rail,
So well bred and so pure.
A horse full of beauty with flaxen mane and tail,
And a shimmering coat of gold,
A nature so sweet and loving to me,
Yet also a nature so bold.
She stands in her paddock, her golden coat,
Highlighted by the moon,
She moves in the night like a lonesome ghost,
Any horselovers heart would swoon.
Such a loyal steed she trots to the fence,
Whenever I call her name,
She never jolts but merely floats,
Holds all other steeds to shame.
She's so full of spirit, she's wild and free,
With ears alert and eyes so bright,
She's like a phantom of the wind,
She's the apparition of the night.
Then as if by magic morning dawns,
And by day she's my palomino mare,
With a coat of gold like a new minted coin,
And a mane and tail so fair.
Oh how I love my Arab steed,
She makes me feel so filthy rich,
Our rides are like magic, as we gallop the fields,
Gliding over water, fences and ditch.

Lisa Jayne Bronger

69

The Horse

A raging storm on a winter sea,
That taunts and teases the waves,
To slap the rocky coast
And torment the ocean gulls.
Can hold no more power
Than a spring-hocked
Show jumper has coiled in his legs.

Nor can the first rays of spring
Coaxing flowers to cast off green overcoats
And display their summer frills
Or throwing up rainbows from mist-jewelled webs
Hold more beautiful perfection
Than a spindle-legged
Colt, wobbling his first steps.

Nor can a hot summer's day
In a dappled glade
With swallows gliding lazily
In still, cloudless skies
Hold more lazy peacefulness
Than two dozing ponies
Nose to tail, under a shady tree.

Nor can the harvest moon
Beaming shafts of ghostly light
To reflect on a crystal lake
And light the way for midnight swans
Hold more pride and grace
Than a horse at liberty
Trotting free through emerald fields.

Susan Murray

Transformation

Black, shaggy, muddy,
The only description that springs to mind
But I still bought *it*,
I say it, as it was hard to identify,
Home it came, wild and untrained.

Sweat, tears, progress,
Month after month,
Something's now appearing,
The work is paying off.

Black, shiny, beautiful,
What a transformation,
Off to shows, winning rosettes,
My new pony and best friend,
Lucy.

Leigh Duncan

Cloudy

Cloudy my little grey,
He comforts me in every way,
He knows when I'm sad,
He knows when I'm glad,
He can tell when I'm happy,
Out of the four,
Is it wrong that I love him more?
Or is it right because he's so bright?
In the show ring,
The way in which he trots so elegantly,
His hoofs hardly touch the ground.
His tail up high and his head so tall,
As I hold him in the ring,
I look anxiously at the judge
He points my way,
Again he's won,
How well he's done
Cloudy my little grey.

Louise V Pearson

A Horse Talk

I am a horse
No blue blood, no paper
Grey I am
French they say
Jumping is my best
Rodeos and flying riders
Are on my playing days
But when comes the 'day'
Serious I become
And rosettes I collect
My Mrs is crazy about me
And forgives me
As she knows
I'm never moody, but just playing.

Marie-Francoise Frossard

Jimmy's Lament

Now alone in this field so free
Do often wonder, where is she
Who raced and played
And stood for shade
Beneath this tree?
Did laze and graze
Was dampened in the morning haze
For summers three.

Her footprints in the mud I see
Where she did wander here with me
Upon the bark she left her mark,
But where now can she be?
Beside the fence I stand, I stare
Whereupon was caught her hair.
Her ghost does float before my eyes
As tears do fall from darkened skies
I wish again could see her kick
And buck and rear and turn so quick.

I waken to reality
To find there's no one here but me
Night and day this field I roam
But guess she must be far from home
As to my call there's no reply
If I were human I would cry
I ne'er was told
But, was she sold
Or did she die?

Hazel McKendrick

The Show Pony

The show pony stood, like a statue so still,
With his huge bulging muscles betraying his skill.
His hooves were oh! so polished and clean,
He was so quiet and good, it was like riding a dream.
His saddle was gleaming, so soft and new,
A rosette on his bridle, cottony blue.
His mahogany coat gleamed in the sun,
He carried his head proudly, pleased that he'd won.

Sarah Bushe

A Wonderful Gift

(To Quisto, her filly Arli, and their owner Ciara
That wonderful gift has come)

A wonderful thing is nature.
A wonderful thing is the Horse.
Put nature and the horse together,
And the wonderful gift is born.

Her coat was silky smooth.
Her little legs trembled.
Her huge eyes shone.
As her new life begun.

Her Mum looked on with pride.
That pride was in her heart.
What gift was her filly.
As only a Mum could wish.

A wonderful gift was Quisto.
A wonderful gift was Arli.
Put nature and the horse together,
And that Wonderful Gift is born.

Karen O'Driscoll

The Foal

The night is long,
The straw is soft,
I know tonight it's time,
I'm frightened
I'm restless
My friends snort silently in
The darkness,
Giving me comfort,
I lie down,
The pain starts again,
I'm sweating,
I'm pushing,
At last the pain eases,
I nicker softly to the
Small shape,
Lying close beside me,
At long last,
The foal has arrived.

Brenda Foxcroft

Searching for Skewbald Polly!

To own my own horse, it was a dream,
To ride over the hills and through the stream,
What a task myself to set
Visit a horse, then call the vet.
On it went for two long years,
Inspecting feet, legs and ears.
I did think I had found my dream
He was ginger, he bucked, butted and was mean.
Dealers and wheelers I nearly gave in
One named Rolly he was a sin.
Christmas at last I found, Skewbald Polly!
She was the one, sturdy and loyal,
Well worth waiting for her silver tail
My dream's complete after a long long trail.

Janis R Witt-Way

My Pony Minnie

My pony's name is Minnie,
You ought to hear her whinny,
She stamps and stamps for food,
Her manners are so rude,
She's got a pretty face,
Everything in the right place,
She's such a cutie pie,
And she can jump so high,
She sees a fence, her ears prick,
Come on Karen, let's jump it quick,
She doesn't like the whip,
It sometimes makes her flip,
Then she starts to buck around,
I sometimes end up on the ground,
At the end of the day, I feed her hay,
I give her a thick straw bed,
She really is well fed,
I say 'goodnight' to Minnie,
You ought to hear her whinny.

Karen Bosworth

Let us Salute the Horse!

Let us salute the horse!
Through the ages he has worked hard for man.
He has been willing, yet kept his proud heart.
He has pulled heavy loads, much heavier than himself;
He has jumped high fences, much higher than himself;
He has been asked to race faster and faster
For man's selfish greed,
Yet he has remained our faithful, trusting friend
Through the generations.
Let us always remember to treat him with respect;
Let us always see to his needs before our own;
Let us allow him a peaceful retirement
When his working days are over.
And, above all, let us return the love
He so freely gives and so richly deserves
- Our friend, the horse.

Liz Morrison

Misty the Race Horse

Misty the race horse
Was never a disgrace
She would gallop with force
With a wild looking face.

Crossing the countryside
And along marsh grass
Cantering with such pride
Misty would silently pass.

One day the Heavens opened
Her tail waved to and fro
Misty nervously revealed
I released her reins and let her go.

I had to work with quick impulsion
To keep control of misty
It was one of a rare occasion
When she reacted rather jumpy.

Misty strides with such excellence
Her performance is eminent worth
She has never faulted her intelligence
From the day she had her birth.

Sarah Whitehead

Galloping . . .

Gallop for me,
Horse of the wilds,
Gallop on . . .

Gallop on the wind,
For you are the wind.

Mysterious and mystic,
You gallop on . . .
Horse of fire.

Your beauty has no equal,
For you are beauty in itself . . .

Samantha Rodwell

The Jumping Two

Crispin and Whizz,
Crispin and Whizz jumping the course at Wembley,
Jump, jump, jump is all they do,
Jumping at Newark and Stonliegh too,
Watch out! Here comes Whizz,
Clears the triple bar not to fall and carries on,
Ascending the water slips but gallops on,
Not far behind Crispin flies,
Jumps flat but clears by far,
The jumps are six foot ten but they don't seem to care!
With determination they carry on,
The crowd sit tight,
Waiting tensed, to cheer them on,
They jump the wall,
One more to go,
As they take off and land to clear the planks,
The crowd rises and cheers,
You are the champs!
You are the champs!

Jaime Towers

Thomas

It was time to buy my only thing that I had longed for,
A close friend that I would do anything for,
I looked and looked but I could not see
anything that was pleasing to me,
I saw big horses, small horses, fat horses, wild horses
but to handle some of these I would have to go on riding courses,
Until one skinny horse caught my eye
I thought to myself I, I,
He was not much to look at but to me he was the one
he was gentle kind and pretty definitely number one
he was not expensive nor cheap but I knew that I had
saved him from the scrap heap,
I took him home and loved him dearly
and thought to myself you died nearly
people laughed when they saw my Thomas
one shouted I'll give it a week
it'll be dead, honest,
But I looked at them and said no way
my Thomas is here and he is here to stay
It's been five months now that I've had Thomas
He's a real beauty now that's a promise
I keep saying to myself he's all mine
All it took was love patience and time
So you see any one can get a great bargain
Just like me.

Michelle Ball

He's Gem (a Tribute)

He's old and aged,
But he's him,
I would not change him for the world,
He's been with me a long time now,
You could say he's partly my world.

He's served me well over the years,
We've had our ups and downs,
Tantrums and pleasures,
He loves to play the clown.

He's still got all his faculties,
An eye for the ladies too,
Only to be caught when he wants,
But love him 'I do!'

He's been with me for twenty years now,
And is going on forty-five,
I'm going to have a party so I can shout out loud,
'I love you Gem and thank you for all the pleasure you bring,'
I'll raise my glass and toast that you'll have many more of these,
Thanks Gem for just being you.

Elaine Bird

Day One

'Good morning, here's your mount, this is Toffee,
don't be afraid, she's a lovely pony.'
In looks maybe, certainly not nature, by the end of day one, I needed
more than strong coffee
She had appeared so pitiful, so lonely.

'Don't worry Toffee, I love you'
then foolishly proceeded to give her a big hug,
Showing her appreciation, I received a sinking bite, which
immediately turned blue,
She was without a doubt a true seasoned thug.

The lesson progressed and finally time to trot.
I proceeded in displaying my unique technique - Toffee of course
disagreed.
After a very brief flying lesson I landed - plot
'Someone swap ponies with me Please!'

'Now after every ride you must be certain your ponies feet are clean'
Toffee, overeager to display her immaculately clean feet,
sent her hindfoot right into my face - that I decided was mean,
and I retired quite willing to admit defeat.

Other people say their experiences were bliss,
something never to be forgotten.
I can assure you - I could have given mine a miss,
but I must confess day one has never been forgotten.

Sharon Kerr

Dancing Willow - What a Nice Name!

Dancing Willow - what a nice name! It is a pity that he's not the same
As the Arabs on posters in most magazines, he won't even canter if
he wants to wee!
Trotting along with his head in the air, not on the bit with lots of flair,
Stands in the corner and gets beaten up - come on Willow, pull your
socks up!

He jumps very well up to two feet six, much bigger than that
and he says, 'Hey what's this!'
He's good in the box though, except with another, when he gets so
upset and all in a bother.
With his tail held high and his nostrils aglare, people stare at
shows saying, 'What have you got there?'
But he's my grey Arab and I'm actually proud - even if he is just a
little bit loud.

His good points are few and far between, but when doing games
, we're a right good team,
He's quick off the mark and easy to stop and when the rosettes
come, we've got the lot!
He's not very big, in fact he's quite small but when we're together we
have such a ball!
He struts round the field as if he's real tough but secretly we all call
him the Puff!

He's good in traffic, no doubt about that, when a big lorry comes he
seems blind as a bat!
He loves me does Willow, I know that for sure - he whinnies to me
from over his door!
Six years now I've had him - we're still in the novice! On
approaching a ditch he thinks it's a crevice
He's really quite sweet, I've made him sound bad - if he read this
poem he'd be very sad!

I really must say that despite this trouble (I've heard of people who've
suffered double)
I mustn't complain, keep trying I can - because you see he's my little
man!

Rachel Westbury

The Show

I took my mare into the ring.
But our minds were on other things
'Come on girl, let's try,
We can do it, you and I.'

We did well on the ground
The judge looked us up and down,
But some foals arrived by the ring
My mare whinnied, reared up and everything.

I felt sad, my mare still looking across
Remembering her foal that she lost,
The judge pointed to us, we stood in a small line
Then asked us to walk forward one more time.

The judge then came nearer and patted her neck
'Well done,' he said, and gave us a rosette,
I couldn't believe it, what a day,
I will always remember the 21st of May.

Sharon Lee

Whoever Named Her Snowie?

My horse is a beautiful grey,
But she doesn't like it that way.
In the stable at night,
When I've put out the light,
She transforms herself to a bay.

If I want to compete at a show,
I wash her before we're to go.
But just overnight
She gets rid of the white
And becomes *Stained with dirt*, not Snow.

Before we were showing one day,
I rugged her; then put her away.
But Snowie, I guess
Rolled more, not less
And came out as skewbald not grey!

Why did he let her go?
The person who christened her Snow?
She's black and she's brown.
She's skewbald and bay.
But she's still always *Best in the show!*

Jackie Alexander

90

Bred to Win

Ears pricked, nostrils flaring,
sharing the mood of the crowd who are cheering,
he enters the home-straight, past all caring
for muscles all aching and lungs that are straining for air.

Bit between teeth, still on the bridle,
field opening wide, his rivals all tiring,
he measures his pace, his mind never idle
but thinking and planning, intent on the hurdle ahead.

Full concentration, not even hearing
the cheering, the shouting, of crowds who are yelling,
his eyes straight ahead on the fence that is nearing,
rivals forgotten, taut body oblivious to pain,

adrenaline rising, excitement increasing,
the end now in sight and victory looming,
the crowd on his side - with rhythm unceasing
and perfectly poised he takes the last fence in his stride.

Still on the bridle, spurred on by the cheering,
he responds to his rider, the whip never needing,
hands and heels he is ridden, defeat never fearing;
quickening his pace he hears the crowd shout, ' He has won!'

The shouts now are deafening, the loudspeakers blaring;
he slackens his pace and with feet a clip-clopping,
wearing and sweating
and painfully aching,
his heart swells with pride at the thought of the good race he's run.

Who can now fault him, champion of champions,
a racehorse that never gives in,
game and courageous, with pluck that's contagious,
bred from bloodstock that knows how to win!

Barbara Bancroft

The Thoroughbred

She glides along
As tho' on air
With nostrils aflair
And mane a flow
I stand back
And watch her go.

She moves like the wind
Her head held high
I'm sure she could fly.

Oh how I love
My beautiful steed
She is of course
The Thoroughbred Breed

Carol Jones

Ode to Conker

I want a Pony, I used to cry,
Please Mum, please Dad or else I'll die,
When birthdays came round, I'd use the same plea,
Please Mum, please Dad I'll be as good as can be.

We'd love you to have one
One day you'll understand
To keep it on such a tight budget
It just wouldn't be kind.

As the years went by I settled down you see,
Moved and married, happy filled with glee
Then I saw this pony cute as can be
A little colt, naughtier than most
And with a vibrant chestnut coat.

I ran to my husband, please dear don't you see
He's what I've always wanted, he's made for me,
We counted the pennies and yes oh yes
A pony of my own at long last.

It wasn't easy I tried in vain
To teach him to lunge and long rein,
And when at last I sat on his back
I knew he'd do anything I only had to ask.

He's no Next Milton or Dutch Gold
But he's my own pony at long long last
He'll stay with me 'til he grows old
And when his time comes, I'll see he doesn't suffer
Green fields for ever is what I shall offer.

Hayley Brown

The Black Stallion

As fast as lightening
As quick as a flash
He galloped across the sunset.

As black as night
As smooth as silk
His glossy coat shone.

As long as string
As flowing as the wind
His beautiful mane hung.

As proud as a king
As joyful as a clown
My beautiful stallion stands.

Tania Day

The Wild Horses

Peacefully they graze on the hillside,
Freely they roam the cliffs.
The mares look over their foals,
Asleep at their sides.

Their muddy bodies in the lane,
Their hooves clatter along the ground.
The wind whistles past their ears
As they gallop across the beach
Leaving their hoofprints in the sand.

The herd is free,
Free bits and bridles,
Free from riders,
All they need is their freedom.

Julia Parker

Ecofisk Foxtrot - (or Timmy for short)

The day has arrived.
My one lesson a month.
Well, it's better than not having any!
I look down the list.
Now, which horse am I on?
Oh, fantastic! It's clever old 'Timmy'!

The knowing old bay
Pulls a couple of faces
To see if I'll frighten today.
But he's really quite kind
And no threat does he pose;
It's a game that he just likes to play.

How can you explain,
How the ride makes you feel?
'It's just walk, trot or canter' they say.
But this flesh and blood creature,
A mind of his own,
Let's you slow down, speed up, turn each way.

I try some leg yielding,
I lengthen his stride;
I ride circles and figures of eight.
Three loops to the serpentine;
Now let's try four;
Now to 'A'; 'Halt here please and just wait.'

Why should he do it?
What's in it for him?
Not a thing - it's his generous, kind nature.
All the pleasure and joy
He gives me in one hour
I can never repay in like measure.

Joyce M Hollows

Buzby

There is a person who shares our lives,
A free spirit whose courage won't fail,
A dutiful being of strength and trust,
Who gallops along like a snail.

Like a lake in the night his coat gleams darkly,
And his muscles are swollen and taut,
His eyes are aglow like liquid amber,
But he's a rotter to be caught.

A fine example of a pony of twenty-two years,
With only a glimmer of grey/white hairs,
He's loving and warm and his faith never falters,
But he can't keep his eyes off the mares.

Buzby's his name, and he stands so proudly,
His New Forest breeding shines through,
He'll gallop for miles and jump like a stag,
Unless of course, he doesn't want to.

His mane is russet like autumnal trees,
And his tail he carries with zest,
His legs are quite short and he's getting quite old,
But in my eyes he's really the best.

Carolyn Archer

Horses for Courses

Galloping, bucking,
Rearing high,
A Brumby herd, go gallivanting by.

Snorting, fearing,
In kinked tailed range,
The leader's white mane, tail flaxen with age.

Oh, the Brummy runners,
Much closer do draw,
But one horse rears, its rider meeteth the floor.

And mare and foal,
In panic stricken plight,
The evil lasso falls around their necks,
Only, their too weak to fight.

The angry stallion,
Ears laid flat back,
Barring teeth at the preditors,
Receives the whips nasty crack . . .

The tragedy soon faded into the night silence,
As they awaited the next day,
It would surely dawn bright and happy
With the stench of fresh Australian hay.

Wild eyed stallion,
The beautiful mares,
tending their foals
With all their cares,

In night's long dreams,
Exist a herd of wild horses,
Beauty in reality,
Now we know why they say . . .

Horses for courses

Emma Nielsen

The Horse

Hooves like thunder, pounding the ground,
His head in the clouds,
His shoulders loaded with power,
Large and sturdy, he streaks like the wind.

He pounds the prairie, his tail high,
Gallantly guarding his herd,
Then he stops and grazes,
As the cool evening sky appears.

In the night, his eyes shine like silver -
The grey dawn begins to creep in,
His slender silhouette can be seen,
As he stands proudly on the lonely hill.

He sniffs the air,
His nostrils quiver with excitement,
He is off again -
Suddenly, he is gone.

Caroline Couldwell

Perfect Ride

Unfaltering hooves, sinking into golden sand,
As the sun settles on the horizon.
The bond of horse and rider,
Reaching tremendous feats,
Lost in the ecstasy of speed,
The beach disappears beneath them.
The timeless world of twilight.

Christina Urso-Cale

Back to Work

Horses neigh and young girls
chuck out muck on forks
and brooms sweep, and my
hopes keep rising.

Smell that leather, soaping,
straps and collars, hats
and whips lying around
and ah! that rug now found.

Joy of the ride, come back
chattering, all the time putting
steamy steeds away 'til
tea-time, and the yard quiet lays.

Horses to be fed, their grooms
busy with brushes and tolls,
and goodnight kisses as evening falls.

D Pratt

Dreams do Come True

As long ago as kindergarten,
I wished, I dreamed, a pony,
All thoughts entwined round paddocks and leather
I hoped and longed, a pony forever.

As years rolled by my hope grew stronger
'A pony please,' I'd plead to mother,
At school, to those who'd listen,
I'd tell my dreams of silky manes, and fields of clover, of squeaky
                                        saddles and hay nets teeming,
They scoffed, they knew that I was dreaming.

Along came children of my own
Two girls you know,
My days were filled with loving and giving,
My dream still there and never waning,
It never left me day or night,
But surely it would fade with time?

It never did, until one day, I met a friend,
who said she'd bought a pony,
'Can't keep him,' she said, 'money's too tight,'
I wished I hoped, I dare not ask,
She read my mind and offered.
So there my dream had ended,
and there he stands in fields of clover,
my pony *Dream,* the waiting's over.

Sharron Elizabeth Merrills

The Arabian Horse

Noble desert dweller
Your people saw you
As a gift from Allah:
Horse composed of air.

Magnificent creature,
Tent treasured at your birth
Grace and beauty beyond compare;
But how misleading!

Horse of the sand
Enduring journeys
Beyond imagination
Cherished by nomadic peoples.

O horse of air
Can you be owned;
Held by fence alone
From your wildness?

Horse of my dreams
Will you allow love
To be your rein
To carry me through life?

Elizabeth Fowler

A Horse's Beauty

When he's galloping fast like a swift in the sky,
When he's gliding along and he just seems to fly,
With his great showy head as fine as can be,
He doesn't know what feelings he brings to me.

He's gorgeous all over, and stunning to ride,
His beautiful pace and his great flowing stride,
His ears pricked up high and his eyes bright and kind,
This wonderful horse just takes over my mind.

As his speed and his stamina now start to increase,
All I feel inside is a whole lot of peace,
With a sweet neighing sound that rings through the skies,
This wonderful beauty brings tears to my eyes.

Debbie Gradwell

The Horse

Galloping valiantly across the turf,
Churning up the hardened earth.
Happy and proud, proud to be free,
Neck crested better than any wave on the sea.
Mane flowing endlessly, tail up high,
All the laws of the earth he seems to defy.
That horse, to the eye, so determined to please,
Galloping onwards with such flowing ease.
That magical beast, not a thing of this world,
In him all the wonders of heaven unfurled.

Aimee Gasston

Babs the Best

Babs is brilliant,
Babs is grey,
Babs loves jumping in every way.
The higher the jump;
The higher we fly,
See the crowds chatter as we go by.

With Windsor great Park;
As our favourite venue.
'It's newcomers and foxhunters, on the menu!'
four double clears and we're half way there;
to our dream, made fair and square;
by the *rules*, made to be obeyed;
especially for the *BSJA's*!
but me and Babs don't really care;
As long as the jumps are always there!

Emma Young

Soloman Grundy

He stands in the meadow as proud as can be,
He's my own pony just look at him and see,
His shiny black coat and long flowing mane,
Soloman Grundy is his name.
He gallops around the meadow all day,
He likes eating carrots polo's and hay
But most of all he likes being rode,
But he doesn't like the tacking up mode.
He starts to bite and then he kicks,
Soloman Grundy is full of tricks,
He's one hundred per cent in every way of course,
And his best friend is Olly the horse.

Vickie Clay

Dark Horse

Dark horse and I canter out of the mist,
Dark-eyed mare, glancing darkly into shade,
Fearing phantom-faces, chanting curses.
She knows the woods are haunted, canny horse,
We have seen figures circling the trees,
Riding thro' these enchanted Saxon woods.
Birds fly far, wild creatures scuttle away
At the beat of sometime trotting hoof-falls.
Silent seem the woods, suspended in under
Water green, where sunlight exists as an
Afterthought only, perhaps in memory.
From her dark Celtic faerie ancestry
Some forgotten knowledge stills her fear,
A changeling child, no deep intent can harm
And we are charmed, protected, spell-bound.
Branches overhang the darkening path,
We slow to a walk, our course to follow
To the secret centre of the dark woods.
There at its many-deep-shadow'd heart
An ancient oak reaches high, sheltering
Beneath its leaves two embracing figures;
One, an unknown girl: the other, my fair friend.
In silent recognition of his face
My gentle mare lifts her white-starr'd brow.
Somewhere amongst a pile of rotten leaves
An adder flicks its long wet tongue and grins.
I know the bite of the snake of deceit
When a golden smile belies naked truth;
Rather a dark honest kindheartedness
Than a fair sly-tongu'd transparent lie.

Mary Reed

109

Urgent Journey

An empty field, grazed to the mud;
a lean-to, sheltering only cans:
the pony bought *to amuse the kids*
has vanished since they last came by.

Her unshod hooves have left faint marks
on grassy verge and wooded path;
her mane was pulled by thorny trees,
and fluttered there in the empty wind.

Light pattering feet on midnight streets,
drew people staring from windows and doors;
but inky shadows gathered her in,
and all they saw was the empty road.

Some fishermen homing in sunset light
watched as a shape swam across their bows;
then turned to escort the struggling mare
and help her out on the river bank.

A tethering rope hung slack from its ring,
some wisps of hay were caught on the wall;
the *cruelty man* wrote out his report
of a mystery pony that disappeared.

Next day, Jane stared at her stolen mare,
returned to her home, exhausted and thin,
with worn hooves but pride in her eyes,
as she turned to nuzzle the foal at her side.

Jan McIntosh